IMAGES
of America

CUSTER STATE PARK

Cowboys rope a lone bison near Sturgis, South Dakota, in 1889. By the late 1880s, settlers in the Black Hills and surrounding plains had fully changed the region, bringing to it their customs and ways, and "taming" it—like this bison—as they saw fit. The great bison herds were gone (hunted to near extinction), the native tribes were forced onto reservations, and the ranching, mining, and timber industries were firmly established. In a way, this photograph is a metaphor for the massive changes sweeping the region. (Grabill photograph/Courtesy of Custer State Park.)

IMAGES
of America

CUSTER STATE PARK

Tom Domek

ARCADIA
PUBLISHING

Copyright © 2004 by Tom Domek
ISBN 978-0-7385-3405-3

Published by Arcadia Publishing
Charleston SC, Chicago IL, Portsmouth NH, San Francisco CA

Printed in the United States of America

Library of Congress Catalog Card Number: 2005921806

For all general information contact Arcadia Publishing at:
Telephone 843-853-2070
Fax 843-853-0044
E-mail sales@arcadiapublishing.com
For customer service and orders:
Toll-Free 1-888-313-2665

Visit us on the Internet at www.arcadiapublishing.com

To my family at home for their patience, support and love. . . .
Roxanne, Journé, Kyra, and Fay . . . You're the best.

CONTENTS

ACKNOWLEDGMENTS

I'd like to extend thanks and appreciation to those who helped me complete this project: Bradley Block, Chief of Interpretation at Custer State Park; Craig Pugsley, Visitor Services Program Manager at Custer State Park; Richard Miller, Superintendent at Custer State Park; Augie Heyne, Physical Plant Manager I at Custer State Park; Reed Haug, Operations and Maintenance Programs Manager at Custer State Park; Marcia Murphey, Director of the Custer County 1880 Custer Courthouse Museum; Donovin Sprague, Director of Education at the Crazy Horse Monument; Joel Schwader, writer and motivational speaker; Ann Marie Lonsdale, Acquisitions Editor with Arcadia Publishing; and Will Hayford and Rudy Noetzelmann at Wildcat Computers in Custer, SD. I would also like to acknowledge historian Jessie Y. Sundstrom. Her previous research and publications proved indispensable to the development of the narrative.

INTRODUCTION

Custer State Park stands as one of the foremost state parks in the nation. Its rich natural and social history places it among the most important and most frequently visited destinations on the Northern Great Plains. Located in the heart of the rugged Black Hills, Custer State Park rubs shoulders with several other significant and visually stunning attractions—Mount Rushmore National Memorial, Crazy Horse Memorial, Wind Cave National Park, and the Black Elk Wilderness, to name a few.

At 71,000 acres, Custer State Park is substantial. Its natural landforms and scenic views include ponderosa pine and spruce forests, pine and oak savanna, mixed-grass prairie, aspen woodlands, woodland streams, mountain lakes, jagged granite outcrops, steep mountain slopes, meadows, rolling hills, and red-earth canyons. Faunal and floral diversity is high. Visitors should expect to see bison, bighorn sheep, pronghorn, deer, coyotes, prairie dogs, birds of prey, songbirds, and butterflies, as well as coniferous and deciduous trees and shrubs, wildflowers, and numerous grass species. The lucky few might also see mountain lion, mountain goat, elk, martens, bald eagles and ruffed grouse. For those inclined toward a hook and a line, three species of trout (rainbow, brown, and brook), as well as other fish, including bass, walleye, and crappie, ply the park's streams and lakes. Other popular recreational pursuits include hiking, camping, hunting, rock climbing, mountain biking, picnicking, swimming, horseback riding, photography, and visiting the many historical sites. If this sounds like an advertisement for the ideal vacation destination, then no apologies are offered. Custer State Park is a tour-de-force.

Before the gold rush in the mid-1870s, tribal people, particularly the Lakota, called this land their own. Justified or not, war with the Plains Indians threw into question their legal claim on the Hills. Tribesmen were forced onto reservations and Euro-Americans swarmed to the region, platting out towns, building businesses, and establishing the industries for which the Black Hills are now best known: mining, timber, ranching, and tourism. Over the subsequent decades, Black Hills communities have grown larger, the forests have grown thicker (and less natural), and residents have intensified land use. For these reasons alone, well-managed parks, such as Custer State Park, are increasingly important as oases of natural diversity.

But a park such as this offers more. Its historical context is remarkable. An epic military man, George Custer, and his 7th Cavalry, traveled through the heart of the Black Hills in 1874. That expedition, as much as any other government action, sparked the gold rush and the subsequent war with the Lakota. In a classic example of "might makes right," the Black Hills were appropriated from the Lakota and frontier settlement thrived. Less than 40 years later, a future statesman named Peter Norbeck recognized the growing need to preserve a portion of the Black Hills for future generations. In 1912, Norbeck led the effort to establish a state forest and game preserve in the Black Hills. Then, in 1919, the state forest and game preserve were renamed Custer State Park.

Dams were built. Roads and highways were constructed. Monumental sculptures were carved just outside the park. Tourists flocked to the area, riding inside an invention that transformed the whole country. As the automobile became more affordable, the touring public grew, and relatively obscure locations, such as Custer State Park, appeared on maps almost overnight. The old Sylvan Lake Hotel was a popular destination in the park. So, too, were the Needles Highway, Iron Mountain Road, Stockade Lake, Mount Coolidge, the Wildlife Loop, the State Game Lodge, the Black Hills Playhouse, and Blue Bell Resort. Most of these sites still exist, and still lure the million-plus who visit the park each year.

The spirits of those long gone still cast a luminescence over the Black Hills. From Crazy Horse to Peter Norbeck, their love for the region—its scenic beauty and precious resources—still shines in those who protect the park's environment.

Black Elk, the great Oglala-Lakota holy man, experienced a vision while atop Harney Peak (Hinhan Kaga Paha) when he was young. He said:

> I was standing on the highest mountain of them all, and round about beneath me was the whole hoop of the world. And while I stood there . . . I saw that the sacred hoop of my people was one of many hoops that made one circle . . . and in the center grew one mighty flowering tree to shelter all the children . . . And I saw that it was holy.
> (John G. Niehart, *Black Elk Speaks*.)

The Harney Peak Range, the Needles, Cathedral Spires—all these areas seem to suggest a supernatural power. It's not uncommon for others, when they first see this amazing place, to speak with reverence for the land. Black Elk felt it, probably more deeply than others. Maybe that's the greatest gift Custer State Park can offer—the chance to feel the supernatural power of nature, and to reflect upon what truly is sacred.

One

BEFORE THE PARK
INDIANS, SOLDIERS, AND SETTLERS

Nick Black Elk (1863–1950), an important spiritual leader of the Oglala-Lakota (Sioux), wears traditional headdress and clothing in this photograph taken near the end of his life. The Lakota were a nomadic people, who followed game animals, notably the bison, for much of the year. Their travels frequently brought them into the Black Hills. At age 11, Black Elk was in the Black Hills when George Custer and the 7th Cavalry entered the territory in 1874. In 1931, Black Elk returned to the top of Harney Peak (highest point in the Black Hills) for the last time. From this peak, Black Elk had earlier had a vision about his people, and the sacred nature of the Black Hills. Black Elk's vivid words and prophesies are brilliantly captured in John Neihardt's *Black Elk Speaks*, first published in 1932. (Photograph courtesy of Donovin Sprague.)

This photograph, titled *Villa of the Brule*, was taken near Little Wounded Knee Creek in 1891. The Brule are one of the seven bands of the Lakota (Sioux). "Brule" is a French term. The Lakota equivalent is "Sicangu." The seven bands include the Minnicoujou, Itazipco, Siha Sapa, Oehenumpa, Oglala, Hunkpapa, and Sicangu. The word "Sioux" is from the Ojibway/Chippewa/Anishinabe word "Nadoweisiw-eg." The French shortened Nadoweisiw-eg to "Sioux," a name that stuck. Historically, the Sioux speak three dialects: the Nakota, Dakota, and Lakota. (Grabill photograph/Courtesy of Custer State Park.)

Red Cloud, an Oglala-Lakota war chief and consummate politician, rallied his forces against white incursions along the Bozeman Trail in Wyoming between 1866 and 1868 and won. When Custer entered the Black Hills in 1874, he found two dozen Lakota west of Harney Peak, including One Stab, who pledged allegiance to Red Cloud. Red Cloud cleverly led his people through the transitional period bridging Lakota and Euro-American dominance of the region. (Choate photograph/Courtesy of Donovin Sprague.)

If not for Fred Dupris, the American bison might not have survived. Dupris, a French-Canadian trader, came south from Canada in about 1850. He later married Mary Good Elk Woman, a Minnicoujou, and settled east of the Black Hills. In 1880–81, Dupris and his sons captured five bison calves, raising them and their offspring on their ranch. After Dupris' death in 1898, James "Scotty" Phillip purchased his bison. Thirty-six were later sold to the state as the basis for its herd in Custer State Park. Pictured are (from left to right) Fred Dupris, Pete Dupris (a grandson), and Mary Good Elk Woman. (Photograph courtesy of Donovin Sprague.)

Plains Indians, including the Lakota, depended heavily on the bison for their sustenance. The bison was an integral part of their life, providing food, tools, and hides, and offering a spiritual link to their religions and customs. Although estimates vary, some scientists believe as many as 60 million bison once roamed America. By 1900, a mere 1,000 bison remained. Between 1872 and 1874, at the height of slaughter, 3,700,000 bison were killed. Of that total, Plains Indians may have killed only 150,000. (P.H. Kellogg photograph/Courtesy of Custer State Park.)

In 1874, Lt. Col. George Custer led an expedition into the Black Hills. Officially, Custer's mission was to identify possible locations for military posts, though the Fort Laramie Treaty of 1868 guaranteed the Black Hills to the Sioux. A more clandestine purpose was to find gold. The economic crash of 1873 had shocked the nation, and President Ulysses Grant believed a gold rush could steady the economy. This photograph of Custer, taken in 1876, is one of the last showing him in dress uniform. (Photograph courtesy of Custer State Park.)

This photograph, titled *Two of Uncle Sam's Pets*, is obviously derogatory, and underscores the condescending attitudes many settlers and the government held toward the American Indian. The photograph was taken on the Crow Agency in Montana northwest of the Black Hills in 1895. (H.R. Locke photograph/Courtesy of Custer State Park.)

Custer's 1874 wagon train stands idle on the prairie close to what later became the North and South Dakota border, near Hiddenwood Creek. The photograph was taken on July 8, 1874. In all, Custer, his 7th Cavalry troops, and the assorted scientists, newspapermen, miners, and scouts who traveled to the Black Hills were gone 60 days, from July 2 through August 30. The expedition met no real resistance from the Sioux. (W.H. Illingworth photograph/Courtesy of Custer State Park.)

This photograph displays Custer's "permanent camp" along French Creek (Golden Valley) during his 1874 expedition into the Black Hills. Today, this site sits just west of Custer State Park. It was near this camp that miners panned their first gold. The expedition covered more than 880 miles in 60 days at a cost of $2,500. More than 1,000 men accompanied Custer from Fort Lincoln—near present-day Mandan, North Dakota, on the Missouri River—to the Black Hills and back. (W.H. Illingworth photograph/Courtesy of Custer State Park.)

Custer poses with an old male grizzly bear that he shot during the expedition in the Black Hills with the help of his scout, Bloody Knife, and William Ludlow, chief engineer. The bear weighed 800 pounds. Custer later wrote his wife, Elizabeth, that he had accomplished one of his lifelong dreams: to kill a grizzly. Bloody Knife, an Arikaree, was one of Custer's favorite scouts. Pictured are (from left to right) Bloody Knife, Custer, Private Noonan, and Ludlow. (W.H. Illingworth photograph/ Courtesy of Custer State Park.)

After a spirited game of baseball, Col. Joseph Tilford gave several officers a "champagne supper" under a canvas tent. At far right is Lt. Col. Fred Grant, son of President U.S. Grant. Like his father, Fred Grant favored his liquor. The figure standing at the rear may be Sarah Campbell, a black cook, and the only female on the expedition. The photograph was probably taken where the city of Custer now stands, at the north end of 8th Street. (W.H. Illingworth photograph/Courtesy of Custer State Park.)

14

Custer, his officers, and their ladies share a picnic along the Little Heart River in 1875, approximately a year before Custer and the 7th Cavalry met their fate on the Little Bighorn River in Montana. Shown are, from left to right, as follows: Mr. Sweet (standing), Stephen Baker, Boston Custer, Lt. W.S. Edgerly, Miss Emily Watson (with fan), Captain Myles Keogh, Mrs. Margaret Custer Calhoun, Mrs. Elizabeth Custer (in black hat), Lt. Col. George Custer, Dr. H.O. Paulding (on ground), Mrs. Nettie Smith, Dr. G.E. Lord, Captain T.B. Weir (seated), Lt. W.W. Cooke (on ground), Lt. R.E. Thompson, Miss Nellie Wadsworth, Miss Emma Wadsworth, and 1st Lt. Thomas Custer. (Photograph courtesy of Custer State Park.)

History gives Horatio Nelson Ross, a professional miner, official credit as the first to discover gold in the Black Hills. Ross and William McKay were the two "practical miners" to accompany Custer on the 1874 expedition. Ross found "color"—pinpoints of gold—along French Creek, near present-day Custer City, on July 30. The following day, Ross and McKay washed creek sand that yielded five to seven cents per pan. By August 27, Chicago's *Inter-Ocean* proclaimed: "Glittering Treasure: Precious dust found in grass under horse's feet." (Photograph courtesy of Custer County Historical Society.)

One of the first to agitate for the opening of the Black Hills to gold mining was Charles Collins, editor of the *Sioux City Times*. In an 1874 editorial, Collins encouraged would-be gold seekers to enter the Black Hills illegally: "If you raise $300, can handle a rifle and mean business, be at Sioux City on or about the middle of September." By December of that year, the first interlopers, the Gordon Party, would sneak into the Hills and begin their search for gold. (Photograph courtesy of Custer State Park.)

The interior of what became known as the Gordon Stockade is shown in this photograph. The Gordon Party, gold seekers who defied law by entering the Black Hills, arrived along French Creek on December 23, 1874, four months after Custer vacated the Hills. This photograph, taken in 1875, shows government soldiers in the stockade during the Jenney Expedition, sent to the Black Hills to map the topography and study the area's geology. (R. Benecke stereoscope/ Courtesy of Custer County Historical Society.)

The Gordon Party built a stockade they called Fort Defiance. This photograph may show troops under the command of Col. Wesley Merritt at the stockade in 1876. The troops had marched to the stockade from a September 9 battle at Slim Buttes against free-roaming Sioux and Cheyenne north of the Black Hills. By then, the government had called on all non-agency American Indians on the Northern Great Plains to surrender. Many choose war, including Crazy Horse and American Horse (the elder) who figured into the battle at Slim Buttes. American Horse died at that battle. (Photograph courtesy of Custer State Park.)

Photo-Gravure, Original Engineer's Drawing, Gordon Stockade

This drawing shows the original layout of Fort Defiance (the Gordon Stockade). The stockade was constructed to defend against possible Indian attacks that never occurred. The U.S. government had warned would-be gold seekers that they would be escorted out of the Black Hills should they enter illegally. The Army did escort the Gordon Party out of the Hills in April 1875, but almost immediately other gold miners took over occupancy. The government was only modestly interested in keeping miners out, until such time as they could negotiate—or force—the Sioux and their allies to relinquish the Black Hills. (Photograph courtesy of the Custer County Historical Society.)

17

Annie Tallent, then 47, accompanied her husband David and 12-year-old son Robert into the Black Hills with the Gordon Party. Of the party, Tallent wrote: "There was perhaps not one of us who did not experience . . . visions of exposure, hardships, sickness and even death . . . and the fierce war whoop of the Sioux." By 1876, Tallent turned her full attention to education and writing. (Collins photograph/Courtesy of Custer State Park.)

In August 1875, General George Crook rode to Fort Defiance to confront the miners then occupying the stockade. His mission was to escort the miners out of the Black Hills. Instead, Crook allowed seven men to remain at the site so that they could protect their mining claims. (Photograph by D.S. Mitchell/Courtesy of Custer County Historical Society.)

18

Two miners pose near their wagon and team of oxen on their way to the gold fields in 1889. Even before the Army could force the free-roaming Indians to surrender, gold prospectors from around the country were converging on the Black Hills. The gold rush, at first centered around Gordon Stockade and the fledgling community of Custer, quickly turned north toward Deadwood Gulch. By 1876, the gold rush had reached a fever pitch. (Grabill photograph/ Courtesy of Custer State Park.)

The Gordon Stockade has long been a tourist attraction in Custer State Park. Located at the west entrance, the Gordon Stockade has been refurbished twice—once by the CCC in 1941 and later in the 1980s by the South Dakota Army National Guard. At the time of this writing, the stockade was undergoing a third major rehabilitation. The CCC project at the Gordon Stockade was one of the last—if not the last—CCC project in the nation. (Photograph courtesy of Custer County Historical Society.)

Miners identified as Spriggs, Lamb, and Dillon (in no particular order) wok a placer mine in the Black Hills at Rockerville in 1889. Even before the Sioux were forced to cede the Black Hills to the government, prospectors were dispersed all across this mountainous region, burrowing into the sides of hills and working streams in search of the precious yellow ore. (Grabill photograph/Courtesy of Custer State Park.)

Another 1889 photograph of Spriggs, Lamb, and Dillon (no particular order) shows them washing and panning gold near Rockerville, an old mining camp outside Rapid City, SD. Scenes such as this were common up and down the streams and draws during the Black Hills Gold Rush. (Grabill photograph/Courtesy of Custer State Park.)

20

The gold rush and rowdy times lured "Calamity Jane" Cannary to the Black Hills. Always the hellraiser, Calamity Jane was notorious for her drunken escapades. She once robbed a miner of gold dust to pay a doctor bill for a dancehall girl. Calamity Jane claimed, perhaps falsely, that she and "Wild Bill" Hickok were lovers. Before she died of pneumonia and alcoholism in Deadwood, she asked to be buried next to Hickok, which she was. Calamity Jane died on August 2, 1903, exactly 27 years to the day after Hickok was gunned down. (Photograph courtesy of Custer State Park.)

"Wild Bill" Hickok, sometimes called the "Prince of Pistoleers," and an avid gambler, drifted into Deadwood Gulch in the summer of 1876 along with "Calamity Jane" Cannary, "Kittie" Kelly, and "Colorado Charlie" Utter. Once a Montana lawman, Hickok claimed to have killed 36 men. Jack McCall shot Hickok at a poker table in Deadwood on August 2, 1876. Hickok was said to be holding "aces and eights," now referred to as the "Dead Man's Hand." Hickok is buried at Mount Moriah in Deadwood. (Photograph courtesy of Custer State Park.)

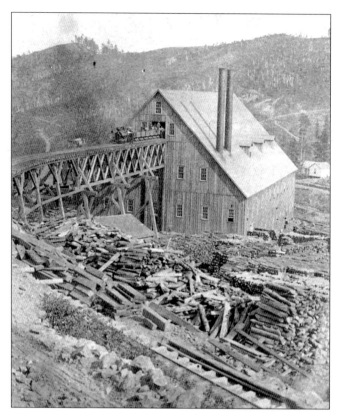

The mill shown in this 1878 or 1879 photograph was probably called the Gold Star Mill located in Lead City, Dakota Territory, in the northern Black Hills. As settlers streamed to the Black Hills, mills were built to feed the immense need for mine timbers and railroad ties, as well as construction lumber for the towns that rose almost overnight. A steam locomotive can be seen pulling a line of cars out of the mill. The mill appears to be around seven stories high. (Pollock and Boyden photograph/Courtesy of Custer State Park.)

Placer miners work a flume in this 1878 or 1879 photograph taken around Lead City, Dakota Territory. Gold mining was hard work, but the payoff could be tremendous for the lucky man who grabbed the right claim. (Albert Pollock photograph/Courtesy of Custer State Park.)

When miners were not at their diggings, they were probably hunting for something to eat. The miners in this 1887 or 1888 photograph taken outside Deadwood, Dakota Territory, are identified as M.C. Millian and Hubbard, but which one is Millian and which one is Hubbard is anyone's guess. One works a fire as the other carries a freshly killed deer into camp. (Grabill photograph/Courtesy of Custer State Park.)

Miners work an open pit near Deadwood, Dakota Territory, c. 1880. Note the men working the steep embankments, their hand tools, such as picks and shovels, and the rail track and ore car at the center of the photograph. No doubt, dynamite helped blast this pit open. Fire in the hole! (Albert Pollock photograph/ Courtesy of Custer State Park.)

The town of Custer, shot from the east, is shown in this 1890 photograph. By then, Custer was already around 15 years old. Even in 1876, Custer could boast as many as 100 buildings. The miners who first occupied what became Custer originally called their camp Stonewall after Confederate General Stonewall Jackson. Many miners who came to the Black Hills were Southerners who came west after the Civil War and as gold played out in pockets of the Appalachian Mountains. (Grabill photograph/Courtesy of Custer State Park.)

Stage lines served the Black Hills region well during the initial settlement period. This early photograph shows a coach for the Black Hills Stage and Express, which operated from 1876 to 1887. In the early days of Black Hills stage lines, robberies were common. Nearly daily, some coach somewhere in the Black Hills region would be held up by highwaymen, who usually lay hidden from view until the stage coach was practically on top of them. (Photograph courtesy of Custer State Park.)

In 1878, a newspaper reporter wrote: "The country north and east of Belle Fourche is rapidly being filled with herds of cattle." In fact, cattle were rapidly filling savanna lands and meadows in the Black Hills, as well, as cowmen sought to produce meat for the thousands of settlers drawn to the Hills and the tribesmen now forced onto reservations. This 1887 photograph shows a round-up crew sitting for grub on the grasslands near Belle Fourche, on the northern edge of the Black Hills. (Grabill photograph/Courtesy of Custer State Park.)

Cattle, apparently both Texas longhorns and blooded stock, herd together on the plains in this early photograph. Note the cowboys at the far right edge behind the cattle. The date of this photograph is unknown. (Photograph courtesy of Custer State Park.)

A cowboy in the 1880s sports chaps with a lasso, and other gear necessary for weeks on the range. Most necessary of all was his horse, a constant companion. (Grabill photograph/Courtesy of Custer State Park.)

Bison on the Northern Great Plains were slaughtered mercilessly, in part to crush the culture of the Plains Indian. When asked if something should be done to stop white hunters from their wholesale killing of buffalo, General Phil Sheridan, mindful of the Native American's dependence on the buffalo, replied: "Let them kill, skin, and sell until the buffalo is exterminated, as it is the only way to bring lasting peace and allow civilization to advance." Joe Heumphreus, Bob Patterson, and Charlie Sager killed the last bison in the Black Hills west of Custer in 1884. (P.H. Kellogg photograph/Courtesy of Custer State Park.)

As cowmen advanced over the plains and into the Black Hills, they brought families and built homes. The 1882 photograph shows a ranch homestead in the Dakota Territory, possibly on the edge of the Black Hills. (Grabill photograph/Courtesy of Custer State Park.)

An early settler stands outside his log shanty, likely constructed somewhere in the Black Hills. He appears to be holding a fish, possibly a trout. Note the two bamboo poles leaning against the cabin at the far right of the photograph. Trout are not native to the Black Hills. In 1886, R.B. Hughes and Sam Scott of Rapid City transplanted fingerling trout in Rapid Creek. Many other transplants followed. (Photograph courtesy of Custer State Park.)

Glen Erin School, on the western edge of Custer State Park, is recognized as the first public school in the Black Hills. Built of hand-hewn logs, and completed in 1883, the school served residents in Custer County, including families living in Custer State Forest and later Custer State Park. The first class was held during the summer of 1882. The school was last used in 1920. Interpretation and some minimal restoration has preserved the Glen Erin School, as shown in this photograph. (Courtesy of Custer State Park.)

A crew builds this ranch home for the Cornelius Reder family. Reder and his wife Mary Goodman Reder came to Custer County in 1883. Cornelius, a cabinet maker, helped build the Sylvan Lake Hotel in 1893. The hotel was an early tourist destination and beautiful landmark in Custer State Park. (Photograph courtesy of Custer County Historical Society.)

This turn-of-the-century photograph shows Scott Durst moving logs cut near Custer with a wagon and four-hitch team. John P. Durst opened one of the larger sawmills in the area in the 1880s. He arrived in Custer in 1879 and, after running a mill near Custer for a few years, relocated to a draw soon called "Sawmill Draw." The draw lies in Custer State Park, near the present-day Blue Bell Lodge. Scott was John Durst's son. (Photograph courtesy of Custer County Historical Society.)

Lumber mills sprang up all across the Black Hills in the early years, and the Custer State Park vicinity was no exception. This photograph, taken about 1885, shows the "Reder Sawmill," southeast of Custer. The man in the wagon is identified as Odo Reder. (Photograph Courtesy of Custer County Historical Society.)

This 1890 photograph shows another Black Hills sawmill called the Dobbins Mill. Note how thin the tree over-story is in the area, likely due to timber harvests. The location is not identified. (Grabill photograph/Courtesy of Custer State Park.)

Yet another Black Hills sawmill is shown in the photograph, c. 1900. The timber business was very labor-intensive in the early years. In many ways, it still is today, although technological advances have greatly reduced the number of people required to mill a log into lumber. (Photograph courtesy of Custer County Historical Society.)

This stereograph shows a railroad employee in a heavy coat checking the flatcars loaded with logs on a stretch of track. The timber industry has provided jobs for generations of Black Hills residents. (Photograph courtesy of Custer State Park.)

A railroad employee rides the front end of a steam locomotive in this early photograph. The locomotive was owned by the Warren-Lamb Company of Rapid City, which purchased timber from Custer State Forest and later Custer State Park from 1913 until 1927. (Photograph courtesy of Custer State Park.)

As communities in the Black Hills grew and the tumultuous frontier life faded, tourists began to pitch their tents and picnic in the forests of this mountainous region. Note the formal dress of this group enjoying an outing in the Black Hills. (Photograph courtesy of Custer County Historical Society.)

The back of this early photograph reads: "Mr. Vallenthine among his rare flowering ferns, a few miles from Custer, SD. Noted botonists [sic] and plant lovers make annual pilgrimages here." Certainly, scientists have been interested in the Black Hills for a long time, given its high floral and faunal diversity and the amazing number of distinct mineral specimens found in its geologic tableau. (Photograph courtesy of Custer County Historical Society.)

In 1890, Theodore Reder noticed a narrow gap between granite outcrops that drained a pretty mountain valley. He filed 10 mineral claims at the site and began to fill the crevice with cement. By 1892, his dam was 33 feet high, 40 feet wide and 6 feet thick. Originally called Custer Lake, the water behind the dam was soon renamed Sylvan Lake. (Photograph courtesy of Custer County Historical Society.)

This photograph, c. 1910, shows lovely Sylvan Lake and the Sylvan Lake Hotel. In 1893, Theodore Reder used the architectural plans of his wife, Elizabeth, to build the three-story, 60-room lodge, with wide porches and gingerbread trim, located at the head of Sylvan Lake where the dam was constructed. Guests could use boats and canoes to enjoy the crystalline waters and gaze at the granite walls and forest. (Photograph courtesy of Custer County Historical Society.)

Cornelius Reder and his family pose on the rocks surrounding the Sylvan Lake Resort, which Cornelius helped develop. Cornelius Reder is at the far left. His wife Mary sits next to him holding one of their children. The others, in no particular order, are Mabel May Reder, Gus D. Reder, Mollie Reder Parker, Theodore Reder, and Ada Reder. (Photograph courtesy of Custer State Park.)

This undated but early photograph of Sylvan Lake identifies the girl as Arlene Neill. Note the swans gracing the waters just off shore. Huge granite boulders and outcroppings rise from the waters of Sylvan Lake. (Photograph courtesy of Custer State Park.)

This photograph shows an elegant dining room in the Sylvan Lake Hotel. The Reders had built a small log structure for guests just prior to their 1893 construction of the larger Sylvan Lake Hotel; however, the small building could accommodate only a few guests. (Photograph courtesy of Custer State Park.)

Sylvan Lake Hotel was an immediate success, drawing tourists from far away. In 1896, conservationist John Muir wrote his daughters, saying: "My!! If you could only come here when I call you, how wonderful you would think this hollow is! It is wonderful even to me after seeing so many wonderful wild mountains—curious rocks rising alone or in clusters, gray and jagged and rounded in the midst of a forest of pines and spruces and poplars and birches, with a little lake in the middle and a carpet of meadow gay flowers." (Photograph courtesy of Custer State Park.)

The Tallyho Coach prepares to depart the Sylvan Lake Hotel for Custer, *c.* 1895. Charles Crary of Custer owned the Tallyho. He boarded guests at the White House Restaurant in Custer for the ride to Sylvan Lake and brought them back again. (Photograph courtesy of Custer County Historical Society.)

Charles Crary, owner of the Tallyho Coach, built this summer residence near Sylvan Lake at the turn of the century. For many years, Black Hills residents built summer cabins in Custer State Park. Although that practice is no longer allowed, many older cabins and summer homes can still be found in the park, and are used seasonally by the owners. (Photograph courtesy of Custer County Historical Society.)

This is another early photograph of the Tallyho Coach, led by a four-hitch team of horses. Owner Charles Crary was an early investor in Theodore Reder's Sylvan Lake Hotel. Crary sold his share in the hotel, as did Reder, in 1896, to J.C. Spencer of Newcastle, Wyoming. (Photograph courtesy of Custer State Park.)

For many years, guests of the Sylvan Lake Hotel could ride horses or mules to the top of nearby Harney Peak, highest point in the Black Hills at 7,242 feet. This early photograph shows a bevy of riders mounted on burros at the Sylvan Lake Hotel. (Photograph courtesy of Custer State Park.)

This early photograph, c. 1910, offers a sense of the massive granite walls and outcroppings that surround Sylvan Lake. The Sylvan Lake Hotel itself was built for a cost of $40,000, including the cost of a road from Custer, about eight miles distant. (Photograph courtesy of Custer State Park.)

Residents of the Black Hills love their part of the world, and why not? It's beautiful. The Black Hills have inspired poems, novels, and music, such as this song published as sheet music in 1907. A few words from the song: "I know you must be lonely dear/Living there all alone/And I'm coming back to cheer you/In our dear old Black Hills home. . . ." (Courtesy of Fay Domek music collection.)

The back of this early photograph indicates that these four men got lost when returning from a hike to the top of Harney Peak. They had blazed a trail through the forest to the site where Sylvan Lake was built, suggesting that the photograph was taken before 1892. The men are identified, in no particular order, as Paul Kleeman, Joe Piltcher, Attorney Porter, and Captain Hassard. (Photograph courtesy of Custer State Park.)

The back of this photograph identifies this homestead as that of "Tom Belmore in Custer State Park," probably taken prior to the formal establishment of Custer State Park in 1919. Homestead claims were filed as early as 1892 (at least in the southern portion of the park) until 1923 when the last homestead claim was filed. In order to consolidate landholdings in the park, the state purchased all homesteads within its boundary. The last homestead was acquired in 1943. (Photograph courtesy of Custer County Historical Society.)

Climbing to the top of Harney Peak in the early days was not for the meek of heart. The message on the back of this early photograph reads: "Going up! Who's going up? Lois, of course. Up where? To the summit of Harney Peak, highest point in the Black Hills." A trailhead at Sylvan Lake springboards today's visitors to the top of Harney Peak. (Photograph courtesy of Custer County Historical Society.)

Frank McLaughlin (left) and Johnny Wells hold some pretty impressive Black Hills trout in this early photograph. Today, three trout species are found in Black Hills lakes and streams: brown, rainbow, and brook trout. Early scientists noted only suckers and dace as native to Black Hills streams. Custer State Park has 216 miles of streams and four man-made lakes: Stockade, Center, Sylvan, and Legion. (Photograph courtesy of Custer County Historical Society.)

Peter Norbeck (1870–1936), a well-driller turned politician who first visited the Black Hills in 1905, will forever be associated with Custer State Park. Norbeck worked tirelessly to establish Custer State Forest and Game Preserve in 1912, followed by Custer State Park in 1919. He also used his political clout to keep the Mount Rushmore project moving forward. Norbeck (left) is shown with Gutzon Borglum, the sculptor of Mount Rushmore. Norbeck was a state legislator, South Dakota governor and U.S. senator. (Photograph courtesy of Custer State Park.)

Men pose in front of their homes near Ivanhoe Mine, where Custer State Park headquarters is now located. Three men, in no particular order, are identified as Dan Wise, Cap Roskie, and Miles Bodemer. Wise squatted on land in this location, and soon discovered gold, along with J. Chellis. They later sold to the Ivanhoe Mining Company prior to establishment of the park. (Photograph courtesy of Custer County Historical Society.)

This early photograph is titled *Heads of the State Forest.* In the photograph, State Forest employees pose atop logs at a log landing located next to a railroad siding. The first supervisor of the State Forest and Game Preserve, George Roskie, prophesied in 1914 that "South Dakota's State Game Preserve will become a veritable paradise of wildlife and a monument to the good judgment and unselfish motives of the people. . . ." (Photograph courtesy of Custer County Historical Society.)

One of the first needs to be met in Custer State Forest and later Custer State Park was road building. By 1918, state prisoners helped carve roads through the area. The flip side of this photograph indicates that this was the "first road to the Game Lodge from Custer." Construction of the first State Game Lodge was completed in 1921, which may provide a fairly accurate date for this photograph. Charles Sager drives the tractor. Alphanso Hitch rides the road grader. (Photograph courtesy of Custer County Historical Society.)

A steam locomotive approaches a log landing in or near Custer State Park. Railroads were integral to transportation of cut timber. (Rise Art Studio photograph/Courtesy of Custer State Park.)

This southern Black Hills ranch was typical of those whose primary occupation was the raising of livestock. Ample nearby timber resources were used to build the home and outbuildings.

Railroad transportation of heavy commodities, such as timber, was not without risk. This train wreck occurred on a Warren-Lamb Company narrow-gauge railroad line that led to Custer State Park. (Photograph courtesy of Custer State Park.)

Railroad employees sit astride a locomotive that tumbled into a creek along a Warren-Lamb railroad line into Custer State Park. It depicts the same wreck as the top photograph on this page. The wreck occurred in June 1920. (Photograph courtesy of Custer State Park.)

A lone bison bull stands atop a knob in 1902 on the James "Scotty" Phillip ranch west of Fort Pierre, South Dakota. "Scotty" Phillip purchased approximately 50 bison from the Fred Dupris estate after Dupris died in 1898. Dupris and his sons had raised the buffalo on their ranch on the Cheyenne River Indian Reservation, having captured five in 1880-81. (P.H. Kellogg photograph/Courtesy of Custer State Park.)

Three years after Scotty Phillip (right) died in 1911, 36 Phillip bison were sold to the State Game Preserve (later Custer State Park) in December 1914, including six bulls, 18 cows, and 12 calves. Natural reproduction and additional purchases grew the park's buffalo herd to approximately 2,500 by the 1960s. (Photograph courtesy of Custer State Park.)

After purchasing Dupris' buffalo herd, Phillip attempted to move many of the buffalo in 1904 toward railway lines that would take them to his ranch outside Fort Pierre, South Dakota. Some of the buffalo, however, were less than cooperative. Phillip then organized a hunt, inviting South Dakota Governor Charles Herreid, area cowboys, and Cheyenne River Sioux. In this 1904 photograph, Phillip (left) stands with Gov. Herreid over a bull they shot near Cherry Creek on that hunt. (P.H. Kellogg photograph/Courtesy of Custer State Park.)

This undated but early photograph shows two of the Dupris buffalo pulling a buggy on the Scotty Phillip Ranch west of Fort Pierre, South Dakota. The back of the photograph identifies the buggy riders as possibly George and Jess Powell. Rod Phillip, son of Scotty Phillip, is shown standing. (Photograph courtesy of Donovin Sprague.)

Four people inspect the Scotty Phillip bison herd on his ranch in this undated photograph. They are riding in a pre-1910 touring car. (Photograph courtesy of Custer State Park.)

Workers load a frozen buffalo bull from the Scotty Phillip herd into a railroad freight car in this early but undated photograph. The term "buffalo" comes from "les boeufs," which French explorers gave to oxen and beef cattle. The word stuck with regard to the American bison, which is not a true buffalo. The term "buffalo" gained common currency in the language by the mid-1800s. (Photograph courtesy of Custer State Park.)

no.1663. "Our girls (mica mine#1)near Custer, S.D.

This undated photograph is titled *Our Girls* and was taken outside the Mica Mine #1, also known as the New York Mine, southwest of Custer, South Dakota. Many women were hired to sort, wash, and grade mica, a mineral mined in the Black Hills and used for a variety of purposes, including insulation. (Photograph courtesy of Custer County Historical Society.)

Miners pose inside the New York Mine. The mine operated from at least 1906 to 1911. Following the discovery of large quantities of mica around Custer in 1879, Custer became the center of mica mining in the Black Hills. The back of this photograph identifies two of the men. Standing at left is William Garfield Thompson. Standing at right is Calvin Miles. (Photograph courtesy of Custer County Historical Society.)

In 1914, the State Game Preserve (later Custer State Park) purchased 25 Rocky Mountain elk from Idaho and Wyoming and introduced them into the preserve. The Rocky Mountain elk replaced the Manitoban elk, a native subspecies that had vanished in the Black Hills due to hunting. By the late 1800s, grizzly bears, black bears, and timber wolves had also mostly disappeared from the region. (Photograph courtesy of Custer State Park.)

In 1916, the state introduced a dozen pronghorn into the State Game Preserve (later Custer State Park). At the time, few pronghorn were left in or around the Black Hills, and were, in fact, facing near extinction in North America. Many people refer to the pronghorn as the "pronghorn antelope," though the pronghorn is not a true antelope. (Photograph courtesy of Custer State Park.)

Three adventurers rest atop a rock outcrop in the central Black Hills. The back of the photograph reads: "We had grapes for dessert which must needs be eaten on the brink of a convenient precipice." The people (no order indicated) are identified as Mr. and Mrs. Gray and Mrs. Leota. The photograph is dated October 1918. (Photograph courtesy of Custer State Park.)

A tiny figure, a fisherman, can be seen near the center of this undated photograph along a Black Hills stream, possibly in Custer State Park. Quality fishing, especially for trout, has long drawn visitors to Custer State Park. (Photograph courtesy of Custer State Park.)

Two

1919 TO 1946
THE EARLY YEARS

Two unidentified women in this undated photograph pose alongside a tunnel blasted through solid granite on the Needles Highway in Custer State Park. After Custer State Forest and the Game Preserve were renamed Custer State Park in 1919, building and infrastructure improvements accelerated. Newly conceived roads and highways, resorts and lodges, campgrounds and picnic grounds, and lakes and monuments all served to boost the Black Hills tourism industry. Americans had discovered the joys of automobile travel like never before and were eager to drive their families to previously inaccessible scenic destinations. (Photograph courtesy of Custer State Park.)

Americans have always loved their automobiles. In this photograph, travelers negotiate a hairpin curve, probably on State Highway 89 in the extreme northwestern corner of the park below Sylvan Lake. (Photograph courtesy of Custer State Park.)

A motorist enters an old gate into Custer State Park in this undated photograph. By 1921, at least 80,000 people visited the park, a number that seems small compared to the million-plus who enter the park each year today. (Photograph courtesy of Custer State Park.)

In January 1921, Hans Grieves tried to move the pavilion at Sylvan Lake Hotel across the ice of Sylvan Lake. Unfortunately, the ice gave way and the pavilion sunk part way into the bone-chilling waters. The following month, the pavilion was pulled to the shore, but it was never restored. This photograph shows the pavilion partly submerged in the lake. The one person identified in this photograph is Jas McKenna, standing. (Photograph courtesy of Custer County Historical Society.)

This early postcard provides a view of the many granite spires near Sylvan Lake. The card places the elevation of Sylvan Lake at 8,000 feet. Not so. Harney Peak, which lords over every point in the Black Hills, is only 7,242 feet high. Sylvan Lake sits far below the peak. Using an aneroid barometer, Col. William Ludlow, with the 1875 Custer expedition, had placed Harney Peak at 9,700 feet. (Postcard from the author's collection.)

This photograph from the 1920s is titled *Tent Row at Camp Galena*, an early campground site. Camp Galena was located near the old Ivanhoe Mine site and behind the park headquarters. The park headquarters is still located at the site. (Rise photograph/Courtesy of Custer State Park.)

A family picnics near their campsite in Custer State Park in the 1930s. The automobile is of 1920 vintage. (Photograph courtesy of Custer State Park.)

Lake Doran, later renamed Stockade Lake, reflects its shoreline trees in the photograph, dated July 15, 1935. CCCs from Camp Doran constructed the dam creating the lake in the 1930s. The photograph was taken from near the west entrance to the park. (Photograph courtesy of Custer State Park.)

A construction crew, possibly CCCs, take a break from building a road in Custer State Park in the 1930s. (Photograph courtesy of Custer State Park.)

The Cecil C. Gideon family and friends pose for a photograph outside their tent in Custer State Park in 1921. The Gideons lived in the tent through the winter while C.C. Gideon supervised the construction of the State Game Lodge in the park. Shown are, from left to right: Mildred Gideon, Elizabeth Gideon, an unidentified neighbor girl, Mrs. Elma Mary Gideon, and Milton Charles. The Gideon family moved into the Game Lodge after its completion. (Photograph courtesy of Custer State Park.)

In 1918, the State Game Commission voted to create a meeting place in the State Game Preserve. Cecil C. Gideon was given the task to design and build the State Game Lodge. The first Game Lodge was completed in 1921; however, fire destroyed it (under suspicious circumstances) just 72 days later. The Game Lodge was rebuilt and re-opened in 1922. (Photograph courtesy of Custer State Park.)

This photograph shows the dining room inside the State Game Lodge. An upright piano can be seen at the extreme right. C.C. Gideon was the lodge host until 1945. (Photograph courtesy of Custer State Park.)

The State Game Lodge and nearby grounds are seen from this bird's-eye view up-slope on a nearby mountain. Originally, the state built the Game Lodge for use by state officials. With an increase in tourism, however, the state reconsidered its exclusive use and opened the Game Lodge to tourists. (Canedy photograph/Courtesy of Custer State Park.)

A motorist crosses a native-rock bridge over French Creek near the State Game Lodge, *c.* 1928. Native stone was also used in the construction of the State Game Lodge. (Photograph courtesy of Custer State Park.)

Vehicles owned by park visitors line the drive to the State Game Lodge in this early photograph. The State Game Lodge is located a few miles from the east entrance to the park. (Canedy photograph/Courtesy of Custer State Park.)

In 1922, the state added eight Rocky Mountain bighorn sheep to the park. The Audubon bighorn sheep, likely a subspecies of the Rocky Mountain bighorn, was native to the Black Hills, but the last one vanished from the Black Hills by 1880. Some years later, the last Audubon bighorn was killed in the North Dakota badlands and the species (or subspecies) was gone forever. Today, the Rocky Mountain bighorn is firmly established in the park. (Photograph courtesy of Custer State Park.)

Custer State Park opened a zoo east of the State Game Lodge in the early 1920s. In 1923, a hole was blasted into rock to create a den for a female bear. By the 1930s, the zoo had six bears. Other zoo animals included wolves, raccoons, and porcupines. (Photograph courtesy of Custer State Park.)

In 1924, six mountain goats transported from Alberta escaped from their fenced enclosure in Custer State Park. The mountain goats were never recaptured; however, they thrived and populated the park and areas outside the park, including the Mount Rushmore area. These two mountain goats overlook tourists in Spearfish Canyon nearly 80 years later. Today, there are approximately 400 mountain goats in the Black Hills. (Photograph by the author.)

Burros were introduced into Custer State Park in 1927. These pack animals carried early tourists to the top of Harney Peak, located just outside Custer State Park in the Black Elk Wilderness. In this photograph, South Dakota Governor Peter Norbeck holds the bridle for his friend Clyde Jones, who sits atop a burro. The other rider is unidentified. (Photograph courtesy of Custer State Park.)

The Needle's Eye is a natural opening in a towering granite spire above Sylvan Lake on the Needles Highway. It is one of the most photographed features in the park. Famed architect Frank Lloyd Wright visited the park in 1936 and called the Needles "an endless supernatural world more spiritual than Earth. . . ." (Stevens photograph/Courtesy of Custer State Park.)

Cathedral Spires is one of the most awe-inspiring visual sites in Custer State Park. This view is from the Needles Highway. One small stand of 400 limber pine grow in the Cathedral Spires area, the only limber pine found in the Black Hills. Although common in the Rocky Mountains, limber pine in the Black Hills is rare. The Black Hills stand may be all that remains of a sweeping forest of limber pine that covered much of the Black Hills thousands of years ago. (Stevens photograph/Courtesy of Custer State Park.)

Tourists pose along one of several tunnels on the Needles Highway. The Needles Highway and its tunnels are a tribute to the hard labor of many dedicated workers. Peter Norbeck turned to civil engineer Scovel Johnson to build the highway. When Norbeck asked the engineer if the highway could be built, Johnson replied, "If you furnish me with enough dynamite." Johnson and his team used 150,000 pounds of TNT to build the famous road. (Photograph courtesy of Custer State Park.)

A motorist passes by a granite spire named "The Sentinel" along the Needles Highway. The highway was completed in 1922 and is a "must-drive" for visitors today. (Photograph courtesy of Custer State Park.)

Tunnels and switch backs characterize the Needles Highway. This photograph hints at the massive granite core at the heart of Custer State Park and, indeed, the Black Hills. The Black Hills feature some of the oldest exposed rock in North America and are the oldest mountain range on the continent. Exposed pegmatites in the Harney Peak area date back as much as 1.6 billion years. (Rise photograph/Courtesy of Custer State Park.)

Tunnel near Sylvan Lake in the Black Hills
Rise Photo
©

Laborers work at a guard rail treatment plant in Custer State Park in the 1920s. Peter Norbeck insisted that roads in the park appear as natural as possible—guard rails made from timber were preferred over steal cables and concrete. (Photograph courtesy of Custer State Park.)

Needles, On the Needles Hiway
Custer State Park.
Publication Rights Reserved by
Canedy's Camera Shop

Scovel Johnson described the terrain along the Needles Highway as a "miniature kingdom of perpendicular cliffs and canyoned waterfalls." The 14-mile highway was built for just under $164,000. (Canedy's Camera Shop photograph/Courtesy of Custer State Park.)

LES HIGHWAY. BLACK HILLS
MILLER STUDIO-PHOTO-405

Two women pose along the Needles Highway, one of the most popular drives in the country. The Needles Highway is part of the Peter Norbeck National Scenic Byway, a 70-mile route in the Black Hills that links Custer State Park, the Norbeck Wildlife Preserve in the Black Hills National Forest, and Mount Rushmore National Memorial. The byway was designated in 1991. (Miller Studio photograph/Courtesy of Custer State Park.)

This photograph, titled *Switch Back*, offers a panoramic view of the Black Hills' "crystalline granite core," along the Needles Highway. The Needles Highway varies in height from 4,700 feet to 6,400 feet. (Lease photograph/Courtesy of Custer State Park.)

A portion of the Needles Highway can be seen from this aerial shot titled *Birdseye View of Needles Road*. Note the prolific protrusions of granite outcrops and spires and the twisting nature of the road. Peter Norbeck once said of the park's road system, "You're not supposed to drive here at 60 miles per hour. To do the scenery half justice, people should drive at 20 or under; to do it full justice, they should get out and walk." (Rise photograph/Courtesy of Custer State Park)

In 1920, Custer State Park purchased the Sylvan Lake Hotel from J.C. Spencer for $38,000. One year earlier, the state had acquired the lands around the lake from the federal government. Perhaps this photograph shows wash day at the hotel. Note the linens hanging above the second-floor railing. (Photograph courtesy of Custer County Historical Society.)

Sylvan Lake wears a white blanket of snow in the photograph, c. 1920. Note that the pavilion is located to the right of the hotel. In earlier years, the pavilion was located in front of the hotel. (Photograph courtesy of Custer County Historical Society.)

Kathleen Snartz sent this black-and-white postcard to Mary Giddings of Fort Pierre, South Dakota, on August 24, 1926. The note on the back of the card says: "Dear Mary—Did you tell me you are coming? Don't miss this place. It's the loveliest anyplace in the world. I'm working here now and will probably be here some time. It's quite fun. Come and I'll serve you a meal and maybe have a boat ride with you." (Lease photograph/Courtesy of Custer County Historical Society.)

The stunning mirror-like quality of a still Sylvan Lake can be seen in this photograph of the pavilion near the Sylvan Lake Hotel. The concrete dam to Sylvan Lake is located between the narrow break in the granite, where spruce trees rise in the gap. (Stevens photograph/Courtesy of Custer State Park.)

This photograph, titled *Laura and Mutts*, provides yet another view of Sylvan Lake, the pavilion, and the Sylvan Lake Hotel. (Photograph courtesy of Custer State Park.)

The end for the old but beautiful Sylvan Lake Hotel came on June 30, 1935, when a fire swept through the hotel. Faulty wiring near an unused chimney in the hotel was blamed for the conflagration. This photograph from that day shows visitors watching as flames consume the building. (Photograph courtesy of Custer State Park.)

A monument to Annie Tallent, often called the "first white woman in the Black Hills," was erected near the west entrance to the park and dedicated on August 28, 1924. Annie Tallent traveled with the 1874 Gordon Party, which entered the Black Hills illegally and in defiance of the Fort Laramie Treaty of 1868. (Photograph courtesy of Custer County Historical Society.)

A motorist visits the Annie Tallent Monument just east of Custer, South Dakota, in the 1920s. The following decade, lake water would fill in behind the monument, creating Lake Doran, constructed by CCCs. Later, the lake would be renamed Stockade Lake in honor of the Gordon Stockade, which lies yards from the Tallent Monument. (Photograph courtesy of Custer State Park.)

Uncontrolled timber harvests in Custer State Park changed with a 1927 state law calling for sustainable timber management. The park actively manages about 50,000 acres of timber land. This photograph shows workers cross-haul loading ponderosa pine on the Harney National Forest in 1925, just outside Custer State Park. The Harney National Forest was established in 1911, but was later merged with the Black Hills National Forest. (Photograph courtesy of Custer State Park.)

Timber cutters use a jammer to load logs in this September 1925 photograph from the Harney National Forest on the "Ovel-gaard Sale." The state's first timber sale contract was initiated in Custer State Park in 1916. (H.D. Cochran photograph/Courtesy of Custer State Park.)

Woodcutters use cant hooks and a cross-haul loading method to roll logs onto a flatbed truck in this photograph. Ponderosa pine is by far the most ubiquitous tree in the Black Hills, and the one most often harvested. (Photograph courtesy of Custer State Park.)

Two men drag a large log on a timber sale in this undated photograph. Peter Norbeck predicted in 1917 that the sale of timber from Custer State Park would "make the property a source of profit forever." The park continues to harvest timber to this day. (Photograph courtesy of Custer State Park.)

Gutzon Boglum thought monumentally when he conceived the Presidential faces on Mount Rushmore. Borglum is pictured here sitting in a sling as work continued on the mountain. Borglum began carving Mount Rushmore in 1927, bringing immediate attention to the Black Hills and increasing tourism. As the crow flies, Mount Rushmore stands only about three and a half miles from Custer State Park. (Photograph courtesy of Custer State Park.)

The faces of George Washington and Thomas Jefferson begin to emerge from Mount Rushmore in this undated photograph. Abraham Lincoln and Theodore Roosevelt would appear later. (Rise Studio photograph/Courtesy of Custer State Park.)

President Calvin Coolidge (standing), who spent the summer of 1927 in the Black Hills, rode horseback to the dedication of Mount Rushmore on August 10. Gutzon Borglum immediately began carving the mountain thereafter. Borglum, sporting a mustache and with his arms folded over his chest, is seated behind Coolidge. (Photograph courtesy of Custer State Park.)

President Calvin Coolidge (right) sits with General Leonard Wood during the summer of 1927. Coolidge's summer White House was the State Game Lodge. While in the Black Hills, he made public his desire not to run for a second term. (Rise Photograph/Courtesy of Custer State Park.)

President Calvin Coolidge's wife, Grace, remained with her husband in the Black Hills during the summer of 1927. In this photograph, she joins the Custer Women's Civic Club board at the August 11 dedication of the Custer Community Building. The large log structure still stands today and houses the Custer YMCA. Shown (from left to right) are Mrs. Josephine Wixon, Mrs. Grace Coolidge, Mrs. Will Wiehe, Mrs. Steve Ainslie, Mrs. Joe Kidwell, Mrs. D.W. (Bertha) Davis, Mrs. Charles Perrin, Mrs. Trent, and Mrs. Mary Delicate. (Photograph courtesy of Custer County Historical Society.)

This photograph shows the interior of the Custer Community Building at the dedication of the building with First Lady Grace Coolidge as the honored guest. (Photograph courtesy of Custer County Historical Society.)

Chris Jensen built the Blue Bell Lodge in 1927 as a private hunting lodge. The state acquired the lodge in 1935 from the Jensen family when the heir to the site, South Dakota Governor Leslie Jensen, offered to sell it as an addition to Custer State Park. Today, exceptional facilities surround the lodge, including stables for those who enjoy horseback riding, cabins, and a campground. (Photograph courtesy of Custer State Park.)

The Game Lodge Inn, now called Coolidge Inn and located near the Peter Norbeck Visitor Center in Custer State Park, was built in 1927 in preparation of President Calvin Coolidge's summer retreat. C.C. Gideon was instrumental in raising the building, which took two weeks to build. The Gideons pose with staff outside the building in 1927. Elma Mary Gideon stands in the back row fourth from the left. Next to her stands C.C. Gideon. (Photograph courtesy of Custer State Park.)

In 1927 and 1928, C.C. Gideon designed and built Peter Norbeck's summer home in Custer State Park called "Valhalla." In Norse mythology, Odin, the father of the gods, presides over the hall of the slain—Valhalla. Norbeck was Norwegian. Today the home is used for special occasions and is not generally open to the public. (Photograph courtesy of Custer State Park.)

In 1933, the Iron Mountain Road was completed. This highly scenic drive includes pigtail bridges, such as the one shown in this postcard. Tunnels along the road frame the distant faces of Mount Rushmore. C.C. Gideon, who engineered the road, told Peter Norbeck that his pigtail bridges were "neither straight, level, nor flat, but a triple corkscrew spiral." A portion of the Iron Mountain Road curls through the northeastern portion of Custer State Park. (Postcard courtesy of the author.)

Early in his first administration, and as the country plunged into the Great Depression, President Franklin Roosevelt created the CCC, which had a very beneficial impact on Custer State Park. President Roosevelt is shown in this photograph from Christmas Day, 1932, with his wife, Eleanor, at their home in Hyde Park, NY. Eleanor Roosevelt was a very progressive first lady. (Photograph courtesy of Franklin Roosevelt Library, Hyde Park, NY, and Custer State Park.)

CCCs build a picnic shelter in the Black Hills, c. 1936. In 1933, Roosevelt said: "We can take a vast army of unemployed out into healthful surroundings. We can eliminate, to some extent at least, the threat that forced idleness brings to spiritual and moral stability." (Photograph courtesy of Custer State Park.)

CCCs from Camp Lodge built the Custer State Park Museum of native stone and timber in 1937. The name of the building was changed in 1979 to the Peter Norbeck Visitor Center. (Photograph courtesy of Custer State Park.)

This photograph shows the Peter Norbeck Visitor Center, c. 1937. Today, interpretive exhibits and a gift shop highlight the rustic interior. (Photograph courtesy of Custer State Park.)

Artists affiliated with the CCC pose outside their barracks in this undated photograph. The park was home to four CCC camps: Camp Doran, Camp Pine Creek, Camp Narrows, and Camp Lodge. Each camp housed about 200 men. (Photograph courtesy of Custer State Park.)

CCC student technicians sketch designs for CCC projects in this undated photograph. The CCC hired single men, aged 17 through 25. They received $30 a month, of which $25 was sent directly to their families. They also received free room, board, clothing, education, and medical services. The CCC program was implemented nationwide and was instrumental in bringing the country back from the depths of the Great Depression. (Photograph courtesy of Custer State Park.)

Enrollees with the CCC build either a road or trail in Custer State Park, c. 1938. The CCC employed more than 29,000 South Dakota residents during the Great Depression, providing approximately $6 million to their families. The Black Hills alone had 29 CCC camps. (Photograph courtesy of Custer State Park.)

This 1936 photograph shows a road built by CCCs from Camp Lodge in Custer State Park. CCC enrollees built roads, thinned timber, constructed dams, fought wildfires, and built campground facilities to name just some of their park projects. (Photograph courtesy of Custer State Park.)

Lifeguards employed through the CCC pose at Stockade Lake in Custer State Park, a lake corpsmen built in 1933. At the time, the lake was called Lake Doran. (Photograph courtesy of Custer State Park.)

CCCs participate in recreational activities at Stockade Lake in Custer State Park. The CCC program began in 1933 and ended in 1942. (Photograph courtesy of Custer State Park.)

GENERAL AND HOUSEHOLD MECHANICS

UNIT No. I – SIMPLE HOUSEHOLD REPAIRS

INSTRUCTION SERIES NO. 7

FEDERAL SECURITY AGENCY

CIVILIAN CONSERVATION CORPS

This 1941 manual is typical of educational documents utilized by enrollees with the CCC. Education and development of usable skills were important to the ultimate success of corpsmen. (Photograph courtesy of Custer State Park.)

This newsletter, produced by CCCs at Camp Narrows in Custer State Park, speaks of CCCs fighting a 7,000-acre fire near Moskee, Wyoming. One enrollee who fought the fire, Archie Murphy of Sioux Falls, South Dakota, died when a tree fell on him. The newsletter was published August 15, 1936. (Photograph courtesy of Custer State Park.)

NARROWS LOOKOUT

= MT COOLIDGE =

Vol. 1. No. 6.   Camp Narrows --- Blue Bell, S. Dak.   August 15.

85 Men to FIRE

The second major forest fire in the Black Hills this season occurred on the week end of Agust 7th,, at Moskee Wyoming. burning from 7,000 to 8,000 acres of timber part of which is National Forest land and the remainder is the property of the Homestake Mining Co

Fire fighting forces on duty at this fire included 1000 Homestake employees, members of transients camps, volunteersand CCC. All forest service camps in the hills were called as well as Orman d m, Devils Tower, Wind Cave Lodge and Narrows. About 85 men were put on the lines from our camp under three state foreman, Jones, Lux and Siewerts.

One enrollee from camp Mystic Archie Murphy of Sioux Falls was hit by a falling tree and died at the Fort Meade Station hospital a few hours later.

Roosevelt plans on making a visit to the Rushmore Memorial while on his tour through the drought stricken areas. His plans as announced will bring him here Aug. 30th.

JEWEL CAVE AND CAMP NARROWS TIE FOR HONORS IN SECOND HALF

The end of the second half of the Kittenball League found Jewel Cave and Camp Narrows soft ball teams on the top with only one defeat in seven games.

NARROWS DEFEATS ROTARY CLUB

Narrows defeated the Rotary Club by a score of 11 to 5 in an exciting game in which the Rotary Club made 4 runs in the first inning but were unable to hit safely thereafter.

Narrows got away for nine runs in the fourth inning on six hits and several errors.

SCORE BY INNINGS:
Narrows;   200 900 0 11 10 5
Rotary Club 400 001 0 5 6 9
Batteries: Jensen and Fredricks
Rotary Club: Doner and Morris.

Next week Custer will be a host to nearly a score of Kitten ball teams who are going to play in the tournament. Business men of Custer have promised a number of indiviual prizes to be given for outstanding hitting, pitching and fielding. The gate receipts are to be divided among 3 teams.

CIVILIAN CONSERVATION CORPS

U.C. 733155

Unit Certificate

THIS CERTIFIES THAT _Fred. P. Rothenberger_ of
Company _2757_ has satisfactorily completed _12_
hours of instruction in _Stone Masonry_ and
is therefore granted this Certificate.

_____   _____
Project Superintendent.   Company Commander.

_____
Camp Educational Adviser.

Date _Mar. 31, 1941_   Place _Camp Narrows_

Conservation Civilian Corpsman Fred P. Rothenberger was certified in stone masonry on March 31, 1941. Rothenberger was a member of Camp Narrows. (Photograph courtesy of Custer State Park.)

This group photograph of CCCs from Camp Custer was taken on August 8, 1935. Camp Custer was to the west of Custer State Park. (Photograph courtesy of Custer State Park.)

This photograph shows a wooden lookout tower atop Mount Coolidge, c. 1938. Engineer Scovel Johnson built a road to the top of Mount Coolidge in the early 1930s, replacing a 1913 trail for pack horses built by the U.S. Forest Service. The peak was originally called Sheep Mountain, then Lookout Mountain (after the wooden fire lookout was located there in 1923), and finally Mount Coolidge, in honor of President Calvin Coolidge's visit in 1927. (Photograph courtesy of Custer State Park.)

Imagine waking to this view every morning. This photograph of the ranger's residence atop Mount Coolidge evidences the panoramic scenery available to those who drive to the top of the mountain. (Photograph courtesy of Custer State Park.)

The fire tower at Mount Coolidge is shown much as it appears today. The CCC built the native-stone structure in the late 1930s. (Photograph courtesy of Custer State Park.)

Visitors scan the landscape below as rain approaches in this undated photograph from the lookout tower on Mount Coolidge. (Photograph courtesy of Custer State Park.)

Fire lookouts had little shelter in 1911 when they were first posted atop Harney Peak; however, in 1919 the wooden structure shown in this photograph was erected and used for many years. Fire lookouts were posted on the mountain from 1911 until 1965. (Stevens photograph/Courtesy of Custer State Park.)

In 1938, the CCC built the rock lookout tower atop Harney Peak. In this undated photograph, a couple in formal dress poses atop the peak. Considering their attire, they must have ridden to the lookout tower in a jeep. Today, thousands of hikers take Trail #9 from Sylvan Lake to the top of Harney Peak, the shortest route available. (Photograph courtesy of Custer State Park.)

Poet Charles Badger Clark was a fixture in Custer State Park for many years. Considered by many to be a "cowboy poet" with a deep Christian sensibility, Clark built a cabin in Custer State Park he called "the Badger's Hole." Clark was South Dakota's poet laureate (or "poet lariat," as some would have it) for many years. He published several volumes of poems, including *Sun and Saddle Leather*, *Grass Grown Trails*, and *Sky Lines and Wood Smoke*. (Photograph courtesy of Custer State Park.)

This photograph shows Clark's cabin at "the Badger's Hole" in Custer State Park. Clark, or "Badger," as he liked to be called, first discovered his poetic voice around 1905 while in Cuba. His most productive years as a poet were in the 1930s and 40s. (Photograph courtesy of Custer State Park.)

Badger Clark wrote this booklet about Custer State Park in the 1950s. Clark spent some of his early years "cowboying" in Arizona. Perhaps his most famous poem is "The Cowboy's Prayer." A few lines: "Make me a pardner of the wind and sun,/And I won't ask for a life that's soft or high./Let me be easy on the man that's down/ . . . And right me when I turn aside,/And guide me on the long, dim trail ahead/that stretches upward toward the Great Divide." (Photograph courtesy of Custer State Park.)

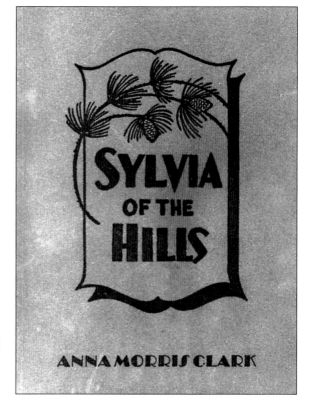

Badger Clark's mother died when he was young; however, his stepmother, Anna Morris Clark, was an important influence on his development as a poet. Anna Morris Clark was a writer, too, and published a novel titled *Sylvia of the Hills* in 1936. (Photograph courtesy of Custer State Park.)

Miners identified as Mr. Heron (right) and Tim Robinson work a hardrock mine in this photograph, likely located in the southern Black Hills. Such minerals and gemstones as mica, feldspar, rose quartz, as well as gold, continue to be mined. Many Black Hills miners recover minerals and gems, such as crystals, garnets, and beryl, that feed the dozens of rock shops catering to tourists. (Photograph courtesy of Custer State Park.)

A family rests during a rigorous climb in the Needles area. (Photograph courtesy of Custer County Historical Society.)

A ranger inspects a young stand of ponderosa pine in this undated photograph. Note that the pine appear to be all about the same size and age. Those who study tree growth (the science of silviculture) would call this an even-aged stand. (Photograph courtesy of Custer State Park.)

Two men work a cross-cut saw to topple a ponderosa pine in Custer State Park. (Photograph courtesy of Custer State Park.)

After the old Sylvan Lake Hotel burned in 1935, Harold Spitznagel designed a new Sylvan Lake Hotel, which opened in 1938. The new resort sits high above Sylvan Lake and was built at a cost of about $150,000. The hotel boasts a large banquet room and 29 guest rooms. (Photograph courtesy of Custer State Park.)

This photograph shows the State Park Office, or staff headquarters, for Custer State Park. It sits near the location of the old Ivanhoe Mine and Camp Galena. (Photograph courtesy of Custer State Park.)

The American Legion sponsored a major project in Custer State Park in 1933: the construction of Legion Lake, which was built on land the Legion leased from the State Game Preserve in 1913. The project put many unemployed men to work during the Great Depression, especially military veterans who got preference in the hiring process. Cabins were also built at the site in the 1930s; cabin rentals are still available. (Photograph courtesy of Custer State Park.)

LEGION LAKE
RESORT

Custer
State Park
Custer
South Dakota

In 1937, the state purchased the Legion Lake resort from the American Legion for $10,000. A restaurant first opened at Legion Lake in 1944. This postcard, c. 1949, provides an older glimpse of what visitors might have expected from a cabin stay. (Postcard courtesy of Custer State Park.)

Three

AFTER 1946
THE SECOND HALF-CENTURY

A bison bull gallops into the auction pen at the annual buffalo auction held in Custer State Park each fall. The buffalo roundup and auction provide many exciting moments, and tourists attend these events in growing numbers. This photograph was taken on November 18, 1984. (Photograph courtesy of Custer State Park.)

This 1946 photograph shows Skidder Fred Babcock and his team of horses dragging a log downhill on a timber sale in Custer State Park. (Photograph courtesy of Custer State Park.)

An unidentified man uses a tape to measure the diameter of a ponderosa pine in Custer State Park. A tree is usually measured at the approximate height of a man's chest (diameter breast height) to determine whether or not the tree is suitable for saw-timber. (Photograph courtesy of Custer State Park.)

A man notches the base of a ponderosa pine for felling in this 1946 photograph. Large, mature ponderosa pines typically develop a thick layer of orange-colored fire-resistant bark. Locals call such trees "yellow bark" pines. (Photograph courtesy of Custer State Park.)

Ponderosa pine can grow to towering heights. Park employee Ron Walker got this 132-foot pine listed in 1981 on the National Big Tree Register. At the time of the photograph, the base of the tree (probably measured several feet off the ground at the height of a man's chest) was 10-feet 9-inches in diameter. (Photograph courtesy of Custer State Park.)

Korczak Ziolkowski began another monumental-sized carving in the Black Hills in 1948. His Crazy Horse Memorial, on private land, stands less than three miles, as the crow flies, from Sylvan Lake. In 1946, Lakota Chief Henry Standing Bear asked Ziolkowski to honor his people as Borglum had done for European-Americans. Ziolkowski chose Crazy Horse. Today, Crazy Horse is beginning to emerge from Thunderhead Mountain, where the carving is taking place. (Photograph courtesy of Custer State Park.)

When completed, the Crazy Horse Memorial will be 563 feet high and 641 feet long. (The face alone will be nine stories high!) Unlike the Rushmore carving, the Crazy Horse carving is being completed in the round. Ziolkowski died in 1982; however, his family continues his work. This postcard shows what the Crazy Horse Memorial will look like when completed. (Postcard courtesy of Custer State Park.)

Little Warrior Pemmican Little Soldier Dewey Beard John Sitting Bull High Eagle Iron Hawk Comes Again

This postcard shows Oglala-Lakota survivors of the Battle of the Little Bighorn (Montana) who met in Custer State Park during the summer of 1948. Pictured (from left to right) are Little Warrior, Pemmican, Little Soldier, Dewey Beard, John Sitting Bull, High Eagle, Iron Hawk, and Comes Again. The postcard was sent in 1952. (Postcard courtesy of Donovin Sprague.)

President Dwight D. Eisenhower was a three-day guest at the State Game Lodge in 1953. The president sacrificed one of his beloved golf games to spend extra time fishing for trout below the State Game Lodge. He is shown (right) with South Dakota Senator Francis Case in this promotional shot. (Photograph courtesy of Custer State Park.)

97

The Black Hills Playhouse draws more than 20,000 theatergoers every year. Located on the site of the former CCC Camp Lodge, the Playhouse has drawn professional actors to Custer State Park since 1946. Actors performed in tents or took their productions to nearby towns until 1955, when the Playhouse was finally built. (Photograph courtesy of Custer State Park.)

Custer State Park Superintendent Les Price (right) receives a check for the Black Hills Playhouse from Dr. Wayne Knutson (left) and Dr. Warren Lee (center) in this 1950s photograph. The Black Hills Playhouse was the brainchild of Dr. Lee, who worked earnestly to establish this fine institution inside Custer State Park. (Photograph courtesy of Custer State Park.)

Custer State Park added a small airport in 1952. The site is located along Wildlife Loop Road. This photograph shows two pilots studying a map next to their single-prop plane in the park, c. 1960. (Photograph courtesy of Custer State Park.)

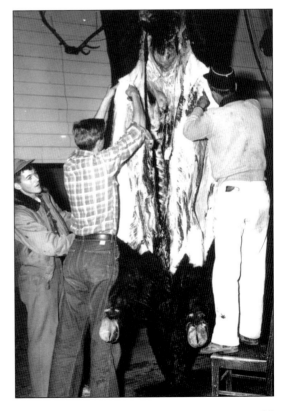

Custer State Park staff process a buffalo carcass in the park's locker plant in the 1950s. Mid-century, the park processed a great deal of buffalo and elk, which was sold to area outlets. In 1949, Park Superintendent Carl Burgess initiated management that gradually sold more live animals to other sites rather than butchering surplus animals. The park no longer processes wild game. (Photograph courtesy of Custer State Park.)

Vehicles depart Custer State Park in this photograph, c. 1955. The park first instituted a user fee of $2 per vehicle in 1967. (Photograph courtesy of Custer State Park.)

This photograph, probably from the 1950s, shows a lunch and gift shop that was located next to the Gordon Stockade. The building was removed from the site in 1978. (Photograph courtesy of Custer State Park.)

Coolidge Inn (right) and the Doll House shop (left) are shown in this photograph dated August 19, 1953. The Doll House is long gone from the park. (Photograph courtesy of Custer State Park.)

Tourists inside the Carl Wiehe's Frontier Museum casually consider exhibits, including a player piano, in this undated photograph. The museum was moved out of Custer State Park in the 1970s. (Photograph courtesy of Custer State Park.)

Hollywood discovered Custer State Park when it filmed the movie *Tomahawk* in 1950. This photograph shows a film crew shooting celluloid for *Tomahawk*. (Photograph courtesy of Custer State Park.)

A film crew gathers images of buffalo in Custer State Park in the 1950s. The park's movie resume includes: *Tomahawk* (1950), *The Savage* (1952), *Chief Crazy Horse* (1953), *The Last Hunt* (1955), *How the West Was Won* (1961), and such 1970s films as *Return of a Man Called Horse* and *The Orphan Train*. (Photograph courtesy of Custer State Park.)

A brave mimics a buffalo hunt in this movie promotional shot taken in Custer State Park. The park's natural conditions and breathtaking scenery provide an excellent backdrop for filmmakers. (Photograph courtesy of Custer State Park.)

Actor Richard Harris shares a laugh with an unidentified person in this photograph during a break from the making of *Return of a Man Called Horse*, 1975. (Photograph courtesy of Custer State Park.)

Tourists depart in jeeps destined for the top of Harney Peak, c. 1963. A concession building and Sylvan Lake appear in the background. Motorized vehicles are no longer allowed to drive to the top of the peak, because Harney Peak is located inside the Black Elk Wilderness, administered by the Black Hills National Forest. (Photograph courtesy of Custer State Park.)

A new chapel inside Custer State Park was dedicated in 1955. Religious services are still held during the summer for park tourists and others. (Photograph courtesy of Custer State Park.)

Cowgirls and buckaroos saddle up for a trail ride outside the stables at Blue Bell Lodge in this promotional photograph, c. 1965. Tourists can still "rent-a-ride" at the Blue Bell stables. (Photograph courtesy of Custer State Park.)

A family camps under the pine in this photograph, c. 1960. Park visitation topped one million during the summer months for the first time in 1961. (Photograph courtesy of Custer State Park.)

The Coolidge Fire Tower continues to draw tourists looking for a view of the Black Hills from above the treetops. Several communication towers rise to dizzying heights atop Mount Coolidge. (Photograph courtesy of Custer State Park.)

The Black Hills spread out in scenic glory from the top of Mount Coolidge. A narrow gravel road leads to the top of the mountain. (Photograph courtesy of Custer State Park.)

An unidentified lookout operator inside the tower at Mount Coolidge takes a reading from an alidade. (Photograph courtesy of Custer State Park.)

Fire tower operator Gayle Huber of Hot Springs, South Dakota, maintains a vigilant lookout for wildfire inside the Coolidge Fire Tower in this undated photograph. (Photograph courtesy of Custer State Park.)

Fire prevention and suppression have been of paramount importance in Custer State Park. This undated photograph, perhaps from the 1950s, shows two men in their fire uniform in the park. (Photograph courtesy of Custer State Park.)

Smoke from a wildfire casts a haze over the mountains in Custer State Park. Fire has always been a part of the ponderosa pine ecosystem in the Black Hills. While fire plays an important ecological role in the park's ecosystem, the challenge remains how best to prevent death, injuries, and property damages. (Photograph courtesy of Custer State Park.)

A heavy plume of smoke from a wildfire billows high above the forest in this dramatic photograph. From July 4 to July 9, 1988, the Galena Fire in Custer State Park burned through more than 16,700 acres. More than 14,000 acres burned a few years later, in September 1990, around Cicero Peak. In 1939, the McVey Fire burned around 22,000 acres. (Photograph courtesy of Custer State Park.)

This photograph from the 1970s conveys the manpower and intensity of labor required to fight fire. This crew is building a fire line in rugged terrain in the park. (Photograph Custer State Park.)

Ever since buffalo were reintroduced into Custer State Forest and Game Preserve (later Custer State Park) in 1914, park staff have worked closely with this powerful animal. Every fall, park staff conduct a buffalo roundup. Buffalo are driven to the park's "buffalo corrals" where the animals are vaccinated, branded, and sorted. Surplus animals are sold a few months later at the annual buffalo auction. (Photograph courtesy of Custer State Park.)

This photograph shows cowboys on horses and staff in pickups driving a herd of bison toward the buffalo corrals. The park tries to maintain a population of about 950 to 1,450 head of buffalo—the approximate "carrying capacity" for buffalo in the park. (Photograph courtesy of Custer State Park.)

Two park employees dash after bison running through a gate in a fence inside Custer State Park in 1964. The bison are driven through a series of gates on their way to the buffalo corrals. (Dick Kitchen photograph/Courtesy of Custer State Park.)

A park employee runs his motorcycle "upstream" on a herd of bison as the animals are driven toward the buffalo corrals, c. 1964. (Photograph courtesy of Custer State Park.)

A red-hot brand seers the hide of a buffalo in this photograph taken at the buffalo corrals in Custer State Park. The corrals are named for Fred Matthews, who designed them. Matthews' career with the park lasted 37 years, beginning in 1954. Matthews was inducted into the National Buffalo Association Hall of Fame in 1987. (Photograph courtesy of Custer State Park.)

This photograph is titled *Two Bulls Eye Ball to Eye Ball*. The buffalo appears to be trying to leap over a gate at the buffalo corrals. (Photograph courtesy of Custer State Park.)

Auctioneers in this undated photograph call for bids during the buffalo auction. Sales of surplus bison help pay the costs for managing Custer State Park. Surplus burros are also sold at the annual auction, which draws not only spectators, but also speculators from the private bison industry. (Photograph courtesy of Custer State Park.)

CBS correspondent Bill Plant files a report from the first annual buffalo auction in Custer State Park, held on February 12, 1966. The buffalo roundup and auction continue to draw a great deal of media attention, including documentary filmmakers and major magazine outlets. (Photograph courtesy of Custer State Park.)

In this 1977 photograph, Custer State Park employee Craig Pugsley plays with a young bighorn sheep that park staff named "Nanny." The ewe hung around park headquarters for years, becoming so tame that employees could feed her from their hands. Nanny died in 1991. (Photograph courtesy of Custer State Park.)

An unidentified man in this undated photograph holds at arm's length what appears to be an albino porcupine, possibly in the park's zoo. (Photograph courtesy of Custer State Park.)

This undated photograph shows the Wildlife Station along the Wildlife Loop Road in Custer State Park. CCCs built the station in the 1930s. The Wildlife Loop is a popular 18-mile drive through grasslands, savanna and high-country forests. Pronghorn, buffalo, deer, and wild burros are frequently sighted along the road. The road received a hard surface in 1986. (Photograph courtesy of Custer State Park.)

Scientists believe that as many as five billion prairie dogs once occupied the American plains. Today, prairie dog populations have plummeted, and the grassland rodent now occupies no more than two percent of the land it once occupied. Custer State Park maintains three to five black-tailed prairie dog towns on about 450 acres. (Photograph courtesy of Custer State Park.)

They don't call them "begging burros" for nothing. These wild burros, usually found along the Wildlife Loop Road, waylay travelers, then panhandle for snacks. (Photograph courtesy of Custer State Park.)

This burro finds plenty of space and ample shelter along the Wildlife Loop in Custer State Park. (Photograph courtesy of Custer State Park.)

Although the prairie rattlesnake is uncommon in the central Black Hills, it is frequently spotted on the grasslands and pine savanna in Custer State Park. The prairie rattler is not an aggressive snake, though visitors who spot one should give it plenty of space to make its retreat. (Photograph courtesy of Custer State Park.)

Along with the mountain lion, the bobcat stands at the top of the food chain in Custer State Park. Both cats are shy and are seldom seen during the daylight hours. (Photograph courtesy of Custer State Park.)

Stockade Lake lies just inside the western boundary of Custer State Park. This scenic lake offers quality fishing for trout, northern pike, walleye, crappie, and bass. (Photograph courtesy of Custer County Historical Society.)

Families are attracted to Center Lake, which offers camping sites, a picnic area, and a beach for swimming. Center Lake sits less than a mile from the Black Hills Playhouse. (Photograph courtesy of Custer State Park.)

Skiing is popular at Stockade Lake. The three other lakes in the park—Center, Sylvan, and Legion—are not large enough to accommodate speedboats. Paddleboat rentals are available, however, at both Sylvan and Legion Lakes. (Photograph courtesy of Custer State Park.)

Two canoeists draw their paddles through the still waters of Sylvan Lake in this undated photograph. (Photograph courtesy of Custer State Park.)

A fly fisherman drifts a fly down one of Custer State Park's streams in this undated photograph. (Photograph courtesy of Custer State Park.)

Mountain biking is becoming one of the most popular recreational activities in Custer State Park. (Photograph courtesy of Custer State Park.)

Two young women scan the nearly inaccessible terrain of the "Harney Peak Range" in Custer State Park. (Photograph courtesy of Custer State Park.)

Rock climbing is very popular in Custer State Park. In this photograph, a climber scales the near vertical rock of the Needle's Eye. (Photograph courtesy of Custer State Park.)

A group of hikers descend a trail in this undated photograph. Custer State Park maintains more than 100 miles of trails and two-track roadways suitable for hiking. (Photograph courtesy of Custer State Park.)

This undated photograph shows a park employee using a branding iron to burn a trail number into a tree along a marked trail in Custer State Park. Some of the more popular trails include Lover's Leap, Sunday Gulch, and a trail through the French Creek Natural Area. (Photograph courtesy of Custer State Park.)

This undated photograph provides a good view of the State Game Lodge and its grounds much as it appears today. Wings with additional guest rooms were added to the Game Lodge in the 1940s to accommodate the continual growth in park visitation. (Photograph courtesy of Custer State Park.)

A family enjoys a day at the Custer State Park Zoo in this undated photograph, perhaps from the early 1960s. Today, the park's "group camp" is located at the site of the former zoo. The zoo was closed in the mid-1970s. (Photograph courtesy of Custer State Park.)

Timber cutting in Custer State Park has come a long way since the early days; however, hard work and sweat are still a part of the process. (Photograph courtesy of Custer State Park.)

A "feller buncher" clips whole trees at their base in this scene from a timber sale. Technology has vastly changed how wood is cut in the forest. (Photograph courtesy of Custer State Park.)

One lucky hunter drives away with a trophy elk in the back of his station wagon, c. 1962. Every autumn, hunters come to Custer State Park to try to bag coyotes, wild turkeys, mule deer, whitetail deer, bighorn sheep, buffalo, and elk. (Photograph courtesy of Custer State Park.)

Living history and interpretive programs are an important part of the mission of Custer State Park. In this photograph, Laura Popkes dons 19th century clothing and cooks over an open fire. (Photograph courtesy of Custer State Park.)

An "open house" (entrance fees waived) and colorful celebrations are yearly fare in Custer State Park. This young man wears traditional dress at one of many activities open to the public inside the park. (Photograph courtesy of Custer State Park.)

Superintendent Rollie Noem lords over park staff in an oversized chair "reserved for the Big Kahuna." The photograph was taken in November 1994. (Photograph courtesy of Custer State Park.)

Permanent employees with Custer State Park pose in this 2004 photograph. Front and center, seated on the rock wall, is Rollie Noem, park superintendent. Pictured are (left to right, beginning at the bottom of the steps) Greg Goebel, Reed Haug, Steve Housley, Roger Steinhauer, Doug Scott, Chad Kremer, Craig Pugsley, Dick Sparks, Steve Esser, Dick Miller, Jim Hermanson, Bill Hill, Roger Breske, Brian Madetzke, Ron Mertens, Blake Clark, August Heyne, Jes Degnan, Gary Brundige, Brenda Hall and Ron Tietsort. At top, left to right: Rick Woods, Rusty Coy, Peg Tesch, Dave Bowes, Sue Palmer, Dee McCarthy, Ron Walker, Bradley Block, and Jay Torgerson. (Photograph courtesy of August Heyne.)

A buffalo stands in silhouette on the grasslands of Custer State Park. Custer State Park uses the buffalo as its official logo. (Photograph courtesy of Custer State Park.)